"Irreverent, sexy, political in th
live performance as on the pag
writer to watch and enjoy!"

"I love the lyrical beats, the *'ola three chord tricks', the*
confidence of the experimentation and risk, the sureness of
self but never pretentious. The folklore and the future, both
grounded and galactic, all audience-participation-ready for a
togetherness we have spent years longing for, written with
our collective coming together in mind. *Action Dad* and *All
The Words I Never Said* made my heart skip beats, generous
poems that remind us that there are no rulebooks for
bonding and sometimes we are all the better for it. From
one proud *Swansea Girl* to another, this collection truly is
just like *Dancing in the Sun.*"   **Rufus Mufasa**

"I am a great fan of Brewer on-stage and hear her voice so
clearly in many of these poems, a very distinct poetic voice
but also in my head a distinct performance voice."
                                    Dominic Williams

"Karen Gemma Brewer builds on her eye for incisive imagery
and her trademark humour to weave together a vibrant
assortment of poems - her second full collection - that dance
beneath the sun. Slipping between startling and sombre eco
and political poetry, and ridiculously joyful nonsense
rhymes, the reader is kept engaged and entertained up until
the last page."   **Carly Holmes**

"I first came across Karen when we were working on the
same TV programme in Wales. She, I was led to believe, the
light comic relief. Certainly not to be taken seriously by the
likes of me. I learnt a lesson meeting Karen's poetry. She is
so able to take a very ordinary situation and give it the
meaning it deserves. Funny and profound." **John Eliot**

"Chants, songs, elegies, celebrations; *Dancing in the Sun* has brought, smiles, tears, laughter and joy."   **Mel Perry**

"I can't begin to remember the number of times that Karen Gemma Brewer has made me laugh or smile or wonder at her wordplay - I mean, where does it all come from? Whether they're spoken, sung or written, words are her friends and she shares them like the seeds of a dandelion - dispersing them like royal favours at a jubilee. The number of times I've sat mesmerised listening to *Blind Dogs For The Guide*s or *Dissident Sausage* with tears rolling down my face are innumerable and in this new collection, as always, there is a counterpoint between the silly and the serious, poems that make you laugh and those that make you think. If you're only just acquainted with Karen Gemma Brewer this is a good place to start and if she's an old friend just let the journey continue. *Verba sunt amici.*"   **Michael Kennedy**

"This accomplished new collection of poetry from Karen Gemma Brewer is a brilliant mix of sharp wit, irony, gentle humour and moments of laugh-out-loud hilarity, all adroitly merged with serious takes on some of the most disturbing problems of our time. There's climate crisis, food security, gun crime, loss of wildlife and forests, plus the catastrophe of UK government, to name a few. Issues around LGBTQ+, sex and gender identity are here too, and personal love also features. Through some sublimely surreal scenarios Brewer manages to elucidate with sensitivity and humour some of the deeply disturbing situations in which we find ourselves as a species. She looks closely at serious questions yet this book is not dark and depressing. There are many light-hearted moments and she cleverly entertains us, so that we can laugh at ourselves and our world, and we can still *'smile, be happy and have fun',* in spite of it all. Just what we need."
                    Jackie Biggs

Acknowledgements are due:

especially to:
Niki, Pat, Steve, Steph, Marion and John;

to publishers of my work including: Culture Matters,
Fighting Monkey Press, Frequency House, Grapevine,
I Am Not A Silent Poet, Mosaïque Press, Oystermouth
Radio, Peter, Paul and Stefan, Radio Tircoed, Showboat
TV, Talisman;

to Lampeter Writers' Workshop, Cardigan Cellar Bards
and SWND;

to John Eliot, Jackie Biggs, Dave Urwin, Rufus Mufasa,
Michael Kennedy, Carly Holmes, Steve Greenhalgh,
Dilys Jones, Dominic Williams, Mel Perry, John Collins,
Rebecca Lowe

to the many people who have supported, encouraged
and improved my artistic output, including: Annette
Ecuyere, Brian Beddows, Carl Spillett, Georgia Owen,
Gillian Clarke, Iqbal Malik, Jan Beddows, Joe Baylis,
Joolz Raven Stewart, Julia Angell, Lazarus Carpenter,
Martin Locock, Maj Ikle, Marc Gordon, Mike Jenkins,
Pamela Petro, Paul Raven, PK Tyler, Rip Bulkeley,
Robert Minhinnick, Kathy Miles, Stephen John, Sue
Moules, Tausha Johnson, Trudi Pettersen and the
really important folk I've absent mindedly omitted;

to David Bowie, Mark Montinaro, Derek Moore,
Charlie Sharp, Anthony (Trance) Jones – rest in poetry.

About the Author

Born of coal-mining and farm-working stock, Karen Gemma Brewer is a writer and performer from Ceredigion in west Wales where she lives by the sea and runs a book and record shop with soulmate Niki.

A two-time winner of the Tim Williams Performance Poetry Award, she has toured two one-woman shows *Seeds From A Dandelion* (2017) and *Dissident Sausage (2019)*, performed and acted, on film, TV, radio and stage, at festivals, theatres, pubs, clubs, supermarkets, shops, colleges, schools and in the street.

Her writing combines emotion and mundanity with a strong sense of the absurd, has been published in magazines and anthologies in the UK, Europe and USA, translated into Welsh, Italian and Romanian, and is due to be deposited at the south pole of the Moon by a NASA lunar rover in 2023.

Dancing In The Sun is Karen's second collection of poems, her first: *Seeds From A Dandelion* (2017) was reissued in 2021 as *Seeds From A Dandelion – addition edition* ISBN: 9781908146083 and she is editor of *Write It Out - new LGBTQ+ writing from Ceredigion & Carmarthenshire* (2019) ISBN: 9781908146038. A first collection of short stories *From Mars To Cilcennin* is due in 2023

Karen is a member of Equity, Lampeter Writers' Workshop and Cardigan's Cellar Bards.

Dancing
in the Sun

Karen Gemma Brewer

Cowry
publishing

Published by Cowry Publishing
8 Sgwâr Alban, Aberaeron,
Ceredigion, SA46 0AD Cymru/Wales, UK

www.cowrypublishing.co.uk

First published in October 2022

The right of Karen Gemma Brewer to be identified as
the author of this work has been asserted by her in
accordance with the Copyright, Designs and Patents
Act of 1988.
Copyright ©2022 Karen Gemma Brewer.
Printed and bound in Ceredigion by Gomer Press
Cover design: *'Sundance'* by Karen Gemma Brewer

A CIP catalogue record for this book is
available from the British Library

ISBN 978-1-908146-11-3

To

Derek Moore

**friend and fan
greatly missed**

Contents

Foreword by John Eliot

Mrs Tom to Ground Control
Mrs Tom to Ground Control
He's left his packed lunch on the draining board

These lines from the poem **Odd Space** found in this collection, **Dancing in the Sun**, tell the reader much about Karen Gemma Brewer. They are funny but they are also profound. These lines certainly tell me a lot about Karen's attitude to society. As throughout the civilised history of the world, we live in an age of heroes, where the sports star to astronaut, are worshipped by many. With these lines, Karen tells us that the husband of Mrs Tom is after all a man who travels to space and forgets his sandwiches. Karen sees the ordinary in our world rather than the terribly profound as some poets are apt to do.

I first came across Karen when we were working on the same TV programme in Wales. I with my poetry, meaningful philosophical and serious, hers, I was led to believe, light comic relief. Certainly not to be taken seriously by the likes of me. How naïve, ignorant even, of me. I learnt a lesson meeting Karen's poetry. Something I should have always known, but within my narrow view, there was only one type of poetry worth reading by an intellectual such as myself and that was poetry from the likes of TS Eliot. Serious deep, meaningful, written for the bedsit and Leonard Cohen on the gramophone. How come the reader may ask had I been so ignorant of *Old Possum's Book of Practical Cats?* TS Eliot's light-hearted but serious view of the world.

Comedy writer's Galton and Simpson famous for *Hancock's Half Hour* and *Steptoe and Son*, the entertaining funny programmes on the BBC from the 1960's that I watched from black and white to colour as a kid and teenager. The characters depicted within these programmes were sad, bordering on tragic. Quality humour reflects reality for me. A classic example of this for every poet is Hancock's *The Poetry Society*. There is also humour in Pinter's plays such as *The Caretaker*, Beckett's *Waiting for Godot* whilst deep and meaningful has two clowns in its lead. Within tragedy there is humour.

Such is the same with the work of Karen Gemma Brewer. She can take quite an ordinary subject and reflect on it. I first saw this when I asked Karen to be part of the translation project with Timişoara University, Romania. One poem used is **Village Fool**, from a previous collection **Seeds from a Dandelion**. The title would imply an amusing piece about a fool living in an outback village shadowed by the foothills of Mount Snowden. Not until I read it and listened to discussion between her and the students from the university, did I realise that it was as serious as any poem I have read or written myself! *Village Fool* is a piece that may appear to be comic but reflects the harsh reality of villages in Wales losing their identity forever to become holiday homes. Readers will be aware of this problem; houses selling in beautiful Wales for vast amounts of money, which locals cannot afford and then communities dying. The only humour here is dry sarcasm. *Village Fool*, who is the fool? The seller, the buyer, the government?

In Karen's work I love its ordinariness. Here from this collection, **Important Questions About Self Driving Cars**. This poem is intended to make the reader smile, laugh out loud, but it asks questions; where is the human? The self-driving car is what we are in danger of becoming, one dimensional and meaningless living automated lives. Karen's view on the world, told through cleverly written humour has much depth.

There is a very serious, sad side to Karen, certainly in my interpretation of the poem, also from this collection, **Legacy Circus**. I have a granddaughter at aged seven keeps my few poetry books at her side, even in her schoolbag. I know like Karen, that words are what I will leave behind. A poem works particularly well when the reader so sees themselves within the words that the reader could have written the poem. This is how Karen is so clever, as clever as the deeply philosophical poet. She is so able to take a very ordinary situation and give it the meaning it deserves. The lines here:

> *Sorrow shared on white in black*
> *Black as tea that's steeped too long*

have as much depth and meaning as
> *I have measured out my life with coffee spoons*

I wonder, finally, have my words served any purpose? Perhaps. Perhaps the question alone has made the reader question, my question. I would answer in this way. This collection from Karen does not need my **Foreword**, unless my words have pointed the reader towards her words stating their importance as a work of art.

Introduction by Mel Perry

Chants, songs, elegies, celebrations; this poetry is full of breath, not just the steady breath of a meditation but the varied and raucous breaths of pant, gasp, shout and sigh.

Opening with **Lunar Seer,** the poem's centred position looks like a moon river across the sea, its line lengths pulse breaths- waves on the collection's shore.   The final poem **Death is Like a Box of Chocolates** brings the selection to its lip-smacking glorious end, and I know that I can flick back through the collection, savour again its delights.

Karen's poems probe a wide range of issues- families, harassment, loss, climate emergency, love, learning a language. While these are popular themes, Karen's stand out with her wry, smile-inviting, belly-roaring humour. She takes banal life-questions and invites us to answer them, follow and apply logic to emerging technology in **Important Questions On Self-Driving Cars** and **Fax You My Knickers** to realise the absurd in our modern world, to foresee loss of humanity.

Some of the poems evoke powerful images of C20th artists, Dali and Magritte in **A Dray At The Beech** and **Life on Marzipan**, Hopper in **Relative**.

Words are well-smithed in this work, images, metaphor, sounds and senses forged by the smithy, landed on the reader's plate. **Menagerine** and **Dray** neatly question with humour genetic modification and the creep of a homogenised world.

13

Not content with writing in English Karen also offers us some pieces in Cymraeg-Welsh, which along with a celebration of the annual Dylan Thomas Summer School in Lampeter for creative writing students from North America and a strong sense of the sea in Cardigan Bay helps to locate Cymru-Wales and this poet in the world.

Karen's understanding of keeping the reader or audience engaged imbues this collection. I found myself reading the pieces aloud, I chanted, roused the refrains, as songs drummed in my ears, and I imagined myself in a revelrous live audience. I was also able to take breaths, dry my tears, collect myself for the next ride with striking short poems such as **Bi Cycle, New Temperature** or **Tree Call.**

For all the slant humour and calls to action there are moments of family intimacy, love and regret- **Sense of Loss** invited me to consider my own ageing and **All The Words I Never Said** is that ultimate appeal for us to talk to, to be with, to listen to those most dear before we find it's too late.

Dancing in the Sun has brought, smiles, tears, laughter and joy to read and I can't wait to hear it performed.

Lunar Seer

Might I
like the moon
be a daughter of Theia

A circling observer
embraced
beyond arm's length

A wan
minstrel masked
turning laughter from darkness

Luminous creator
quarter
slicing life

Sly draughter of sorrow
exposed
to meteor blows

My dint
erased
at the tide's wash

Moon like

Like the moon?

Important Questions On Self-Driving Cars

Will dogs still be allowed to ride
with their head out of the window
tongue lolling and lips flapping in the breeze?
Will there have to be a human in the car too?
Will I be permitted to use my phone
or will that be considered a dangerous distraction
from watching television?
Will it have an adolescence regression button
that can be pressed at stop signs
to make loud engine revving
and exhaust popping noises as it pulls away?
Will the bonnet be painted in a sexist resistant finish
that prevents the draping of semi-naked females
even at a car show?
Will it know the way home after dark?
Will it be unable to tail gates or crawl kerbs?
Will it compensate the last remaining manufacturer
of driving gloves?
Will it be able to complete
the London to Brighton vintage car rally
a hundred years from now?
Will the sun roof protect me from solar radiation?
Will it take the long way
when I need to compose my emotions
give myself a pep talk
or hear the end of our song?
Will the vanity mirror tell me who is fairest of all?

→

Will it go around the block a couple of times
when I am too early
or pull in covertly down the street
when I see their car parked outside your house?
Will it be able to outwit smart motorways
and find refuge in the event of a breakdown?
Will it give me due care and attention?

Menagerine

Churn up all the animals
with rape seed oil
so they can spread across the world
straight from the fridge

Store them in a box made from
recycled coke bottles
to keep tusk marks from your celery
hoofprints off tomatoes

Don't be surprised to catch them
wearing helmets playing hockey
curling Brussel's sprouts
skiing down your cheese

Hyenas hustle aubergines
zebras strip bare lettuce
giraffes butt heads with cauliflower
lions paw raw carrots

At hand in our convenient
domestic wild appliance
Serengeti with an ice box
untamed thoughts for food.

A Dray At The Beech

Sunburned squirrels sitting on the beech
reach from antique acorn deckchairs
for pre-cut triangular sandwiches
of fish paste, pressed meats, egg and cress.
Buttered slices of bara brith
are dunked in lukewarm tea
cradled in plastic screw top lids
from a glass-lined, tartan tin flask.
Dripping lollies licked in lime and crimson
ice-jar incisors far too ivory.
Nut kin swim in fluffy bikinis
surf on tuffets of foamy sea.

Douglas Fir may be an easier tree to plant
but the broad branches of beech
are a better bet for building sandcastles
where tufted reds squirrel away with buckets
and otherwise redundant, dug-less spades.
Egg-stained greaseproof paper flags flutter
from lolly sticks pricked
into misnamed keeps
that seep the incoming tide
as the sun sets russet on coppery beech
leaves rustle in the breeze and beechwear
hangs drying in their tree.

Bouquet Of Giraffes

You gave me a bouquet of giraffes
a beautiful array of heads and stems
artistically entwined in greenery
cellophane wrapped with a red ribbon bow
a sponge at the base to catch the blood

Making arrangement in a lead crystal vase
I wonder what happened to the torsos
and whether their long spindly legs
were recycled as tripods or bean sticks
or extendable rods for chimney sweeps

I direct our display to the wide wooden sill
of a window in the home-cinema room
with its pained glass outlook to the garden
instructing the lawn be unmown for a week
so to them it may appear more savannah

Do you water giraffes I ponder
fearing droopy heads and lolling tongues
or marinade their necks in mango juice
to keep them reaching for imaginary leaves
in belief they are free in a buffet of trees

They watch me sip cocktails on my lounger
splash from a terrazzo tiled waterhole
tennis against the service machine
their wide-open eyes of surprise or pity
unblinking unflinching unthinking un-be

$\rightarrow$

In a jungle of green chiffon couture
I nibble at canapes gulp African wine
at home in their company under a canopy
of what-ifs and maybes no-shows and not-yets
a cacophony of sun-damaged dreams and regrets

At night I can't sleep for their absence
sure I hear them stampede neck and neck
creep down the stairs through the darkness
in hope I might catch a glimpse of their wildness
but see only moonlight silhouettes

You gave me a bouquet of giraffes
but your final message was lost or misplaced
along with your courage to leave face to face
and perhaps in the vase on the sill are carnations
and the sponge soaked in blood at their base is my
heart

Thunderbirds Are Gone

The original thunderbirds
were farting swallows and house-martins
who blew the lids off nuthatch nests
and fired their eggs at sixty miles-per-hour

Captain Scarlet was a robbin' bastard
his song a litany of cusses and curses
warbled to a traditional tune
written by Benjamin Britain-Spittoon

Super marionette strings pluck
commercialisation of child scare box
like a murmuration of off-beat hearts
in the shopping canopy of deciduous goods.

Pachyderm's Top Brass

Ellie Elephant's
euphonium
elevates
everyday
equilibrium

Quackers

Duncan Duck
delicately
dunks
doughnut
delicacy

Island Mentality

Immigrant
iguana's
imminent
internment
initiates
international
in-cry.

Arm A Nag

Should we be frightened by horses
with guns
home, home on the rifle range
from a dream win at Chester
to a gleaming Winchester
gun for Shire on hitman parade

Welsh Cobs with Kalashnikovs
Morgans with Magnums
Hanoverians with Howitzers
Shetlands with shotguns

Up to their fetlocks in carbines and flintlocks
Irish Draught blunderbuss
Gatlings and Brownings, Berettas and Glocks
Clydesdale Colt .45
equine precision with live ammunition
unstable, unbolted with a Golden Shot

Zanskaris with Uzis
Warlanders' Smith & Wessons
Percheron with pistols
Suffolk Punches with Sten guns

$\rightarrow$

Imagine horses in charge
with bayonets attached
cavalry to carvery, ArmaLite then detached
M16, M60, gelding's Lee-Enfield
night mares with Mausers, Herstal to Springfield
AK47, twin Thompsons well matched

Thoroughbreds with Purdeys
Lipizzanas with Lugers
Mustangs with muskets
Appaloosas with Bazookas

Should we be frightened by horses
with guns
neigh sayers' Hecklers & Kochs
or take steps to keep Trigger happy
with nosebags of fresh cannon fodder
and wind up Tommys in their box.

Lunartrix

Down by the river
there's a wolf at the weir
sniffing the air
smelling your fear.
Will you pay for crossing the Styx?
Two shadows in tune
beneath a raker's moon
howling like Lunartrix
Howling

One foot in a crater
hand on your cheesegrater
phaser set to stun,
prepared for the slaughter
knee deep in the water's
tauter reflection.

Down by the river
two wolves at the weir
one on each bank
motives unclear.
Will you play the old three chord tricks?
Two shadows one tune
beneath a raker's moon
howling like Lunartrix
Howling

→

True friend or dictator
our alien freighter
invader on the run,
Theia's tide daughter
silver soul-sorter
quartered crescent crumb.

Down by the river
new wolves at the weir
kindred of wild
blind as the seer
blow away the house made of bricks.
One shadow one tune
beneath a raker's moon
howling like Lunartrix
Howling
Howling
Howling
H-O-W-L-L-L-L-L-L-L

Thin

Bronzing
bold in a
breath-in
bikini a
breath of
breeze could
flutter high
to fly as a
flimsy
fleeting
ensign
flagging
undressed
distress in
soaring
semaphwoar

Drumming In Your Ears

I'm the sun and you're the earth
you're lost in your own little world
you don't believe the stories of your end
heaven forfend

I'm the earth and you're the sun
you think you got us on the run
but our magnetic field will defend
heaven forfend

You need to get your act together
read my message in your weather
change your ways my planetary friend
heaven forfend

It's our place we're a selfish people
more important that we keep all
our investments on a rising trend
heaven forfend

Can't you see this final warning
feel the force of global warming

We invented nuclear fission
so sure to find a safe solution

$\rightarrow$

If you don't finally stop and listen
you'll be missing from the solar system

It's a fight we're capable of winning
if we keep on talking, keep on spinning

Everybody's leaving it to
someone else to break the news
you never want to hear
in a million years

Everybody's leaving it to
someone else to break the news
you just can't keep
from drumming in your ears

you just can't keep
from drumming in your ears

Dancing In The Sun

I saw you dancing in the sun
just a silhouette
no idea what was to come
I didn't know you yet
as I emerged into the light
got slapped across the rear
you invited me to dance
whispered in my ear

Always dance in the sun
always dance in the sun
smile be happy have fun
always dance in the sun

You gave me gold in autumn leaves
silver shining moon
diamond smile, laughing lungs
breath that holds a tune
a spirit fuelled by love and dreams
belief that I might fly
eagle's wings, stunt kite strings
advice when hope ran dry

Always dance in the wind
always dance in the wind
nothing ends before it begins
always dance in the wind

→

33

Winter nights by firesides
hoofprints on the roof
imagination's dance and prance
tales entwined with truth
slip of song, slide of guitar
drifting melody
I see crevices ahead
still you encourage me

Always dance in the snow
always dance in the snow
you can't get there until you go
always dance in the snow

Awakening to old bird spring
in a nest of memories
behind sometimes, half deaf and blind
but with renewed energy
a second chance on a second wind
with more experience
wash old cobwebs down the spout
accrue anew nascence

Always dance in the rain
always dance in the rain
what happened before can happen again
always dance in the rain

→

I see you dancing in the sun
like many summers past
I'll step in on every one
the next might be my last
you lead the way, I follow close
like seasons on a string
spinning faster every turn
you gently reel me in

Always dance in the sun
always dance in the sun
always dance in the sun
smile, be happy, have fun.

See The World

You kept all your promises
tattooed across my heart
held on to your grievances
in recycled
bottles of self-harm

Who dares to shatter unreality
release all our messages
bobbing in the sea
swimming breaststroke
into our insanity
caught in a rip-tide
drifting out of reach

Mother Earth cooker
custodian sentence
iconoclastic
plastic parade
squeezer and choker
bio-dissemblance
see the World
the mess we've made.

→

You crewed all your Odysseys
tested to roll my runes
redrafted your codicils
on recharged smart
memento mori

Unaware clattering reality
unleash all our corteges
logging memories
skimming flesh stones
over our temerity
tort on the flip-side
sifting out our niche

Mother Earth cooker
curse Odin's entrance
missed her bombastic
elastic array
wheezer and smoker
myopic senescence
see the World
the mess we've made.

There Was A River

There was a river
running through here
but now
the bed is dry.

We wasted
all the planet's tears
there are no more
left to cry.

There was a forest
standing on that hill
where birdsong
echoed far.

We cut it down
for direct mail
recovery
for your car.

$\rightarrow$

There was a schoolyard
down the track
where children
staged a strike.

We listened
to their pleas
then did nothing
to put things right.

Crystal
clear waters
evaporate
in memory.

No waterfalls
or kingfisher calls
no kisses
by the sea.

New Temperature

Matthew frozen
cold mark
lukewarm
hot John.

In the Name of the Father

Jeremy's
genteel
genealogy
generates
junket
job.

Non-Stick Pandemonium

Another happy new year
with the Jumblies still in power
our sieve remains seaworthy
'though the water line is higher
the average mood is ambient
a balanced even ire
with one half in the icebox
and the other in the fire
disintelligentsia
in parliamentary tower
too party blind with drink to see
what future may endower
dealing and no-dealing
'til it churns the channel sour
in a world of turning worms
each getting hotter by the hour
we share a petal bath beneath
bright enlightened glowers
of shining sparks
from static bees
in polyester flowers
a new bouquet
nose of decay
arose surfeit of liars
lost giant snails
semi-final nails
no sign of any pliers

$\rightarrow$

do not despair
keep sound and hair
one to one inspire
join our dance
Elastoplast chance
to skip the pan
and fryer

Candyfloss & Brandysnaps

Oh those festive jingles
give me a seasonal tingle
how I love Christingle
I'm an oligarch angel
my Christmas music thrill
five gold rings
of the till

Fill your trolley
join the line
keep in step
with Christmas time
flash your card
buy that gift
it's a con-
tactless way to give
candyfloss
& brandysnaps

→

44

Secret presents
under wraps
debit charges
and credit traps
finance system
on the edge
of eco-
nomical collapse
candyfloss
& brandysnaps

Candy's lost
when Brandy snaps

Just Another Hole in The Head

Through CCTV
zoom in on my name
raise flags of terror
to further your claim
map out my face
record every frame
your bright raisin eye
black hole to my brain
a chip in the block
fishing your game
suck out all emotion
no need to explain
remove all commotion
appearance the same
my escape temporary
won't happen again
forward locomotion
programmably lame
abort every notion
I won't think again
no self-promotion
now all on one plane
value my devotion
new link in your chain

We Don't Want You In

She wants to be an iron lady
She reckons she's a woman of steel
She thinks she can rule the country
With an iron will
She's got us by the throat,
So sure she'll win the vote
Don't you tell me how to live
She's a Conservative

We don't want you in (get out)
We don't want you in (get out)
We don't want you in anymore

Tell you and tell me a story
Once upon a time
That's the tale of a Tory
Their policies a party lie
They think that we forgot
But we see through their plot
Don't expect me to forgive
You're a Conservative

We don't want you in (get out)
We don't want you in (get out)
We don't want you in anymore

$\rightarrow$

They think they've got us sussed out
Say they'll put the country to rights
Assure us there's no need to doubt
Bring Britain through its plight
But underneath
They're grinning through their teeth
They bleed you poor to make it rich
They're Conservative

We don't want you in (get out)
We don't want you in (get out)
We don't want you in anymore
No Morrrrrrrrrrrrrrrrrrrrrrrrrrrrre

Number Nineteen Twenty-Twenty Division Blues

It seems I'm showing all the classic signs of OCD
More time each day on the same tasks repetitively
Gaps between showers growing longer in my soft
shuffle shoes
Got those No.19 – 20-20 division blues.

Keep on smiling, laughing, joking, ha-ha
Nothing wrong here, all right Jackanory
Fear a waiting dark macabre gala
Arty choking land of cope and worry

Don't know if I've got it
Will anybody love me anymore
What if I don't have it
Will anybody love me any more

We're heading out of lockdown but I don't feel a breath
of release
Imaginary handcuffs still bind me to the thought free
police
Mind being absent lost memory phone tri-locked to
snooze
Got those No.19 – 20-20 division blues.

Tell me that I've got it
Tell me that you'll only love me more
Lie to me I've got it
Lie to me you'll love me evermore

$\rightarrow$

Can't stop crying, rocking, rolling, ga-ga
Masking all that I can't face or bury
Shaking hands in cardiogram harbour
Singsong along last promenade of fury

Tell me that we've got it
Tell me that you'll love me truth and flaw
Lie to me we've got it
Say we'll stay inside and lock the door

Black dog on a rainbow leads me rambling from the end
of a chain
Links purring gently with the soft pitter-patter of blame
All that cool cat quiver grinning tonics that no longer
amuse
Got those No.19 – 20-20 division blues.

Don't know if I've got it
Will anybody love me anymore
What if I don't have it
Will any
body
love me.

Down

One morning
I was lying
down
minding my own business
when life came by
and rode right over me.

I was still lying
down
seething
when life came back the other way
and left me
lying
down
convalescing.

Just about then
a passer-by
caught my eye
and gave me some good advice.
She said: *Why*
don't you lie
at the side
of the road?

$\rightarrow$

Well, I was lying
down
thinking
when life came by
on the afternoon trip.

Just about then
a passer-by
caught my eye
with a shrug and a sigh
such that I
felt compelled to reply.
So I
lied!
Very well thank you, how are you?

Bi Cycle

Easy to change sex
if you are a bicycle
just drop the crossbar

I'll Never Stay At The Dorchester

I'll never stay at the Dorchester
it's built on stones of death
Sharia Law is an evil force
in the hands of evil men
if you kill in the name of god
it's murder just the same
Milly and Mo, Jack and Joe
there's no crime in being gay
Deuteronomy is ancient history
we don't sacrifice goats today
Milly and Mo, Jack and Joe
there's no crime in being gay

Woman or man, womanly man
manly woman or trans
stitch something on, turn it inside out,
cut them off or have implants
it's right to be whoever you are
live your life, take your own stance
for personality in all reality
is in your head not in your pants
Deuteronomy is ancient history
we don't sacrifice goats today
Milly and Mo, Jack and Joe
there's no crime in being gay

$\rightarrow$

Sisters and brothers and all the others
LGBTQ+
every pebble that's thrown at one
is a rock cast at all of us
invincibility in solidarity
our mettle you can't even rust
geeks and freaks, one-off uniques
unlost, in odd we trust
Deuteronomy is ancient history
we don't sacrifice goats today
Milly and Mo, Jack and Joe
there's no crime in being gay

I'll never stay at the Dorchester

Monster Love Monster

Two hundred years of loneliness
are almost at an end
I've gathered enough pieces
to make for you a friend
when lightning strikes a second time
the power it will send
a loving soul into this bowl
of ghoulish goulash blend
monster ascend

It's taken me a while
apologies for the delay
red tape and regulation
make it difficult today
to compile stocks of organs
severed limbs and entire brains
but by stealth through morgues and hospitals
cemeteries and drains
she walks again

Frankenstein
meet Fran Bea Stein
monster love monster

$\rightarrow$

We are individuals
every one of us unique
I say *vive la difference*
in mind, thought and physique
whether your cup runneth over
or your teapot's sprung a leak
there's no such thing as normal
only new, used and antique
we all are freaks.

Frankenstein
meet Fran Bea Stein
monster love monster.

Treasure's Hunt

I painted my gender magenta
pierced it three times with a pin
but you turned your back on my gesture
not so much as a bell for my ring

I removed all my pubes with your tweezers
crocheted you a darling moustache
you behaved like Sade: Marquis de
and spent all weekend on the lash

I had two tattoos in tight places
your name and your name once again
but you came without reading glasses
screaming 'O god' was to blame

I waxed up my nipples like candles
gave you the light to both wicks
you strapped yourself up in man handles
pulled off behind the scenes tricks

I fashioned a scarf from your bike chain
kneeled padlocked outside your front door
you insisted I signed for your parcels
unwrapped me until I was sore

I threw down a black latex gauntlet
slapped your left cheek with its pair
you downloaded a double entendre
to force feed your chocolate éclair

→

Your leash drawing tight on my collar
turned life to a crawl in the park
raw meat engorged and *al dente*
your bite much improved on my bark

I bought a hot iron and a brazier
beseeched you to join in my brand
at last you unburied your Treasure
clasped my doubloons with both hands.

Odd Space

Mrs Tom to Ground Control
Mrs Tom to Ground Control
He's left his packed lunch on the draining board

Mrs Tom to Ground Control
I was watching Countdown when you rang
What's our position if you don't bring him back?

J, I, H, G, F, E, D, C, B, Alpha bets off

This is Mrs Tom to Ground Control
I've had the papers on the phone
They seem to think he's been wearing my blouses
Have you reminded him it's time to take his capsule

This is Mrs Tom, again, to Ground Control
Reporters at the door
No weight to their peculiar accusations
What do you mean he's stepped out of the office?

Here's me
Sitting in our council terrace
on top of the hill
feeling very blue
now I'm earth bound without you

$\rightarrow$

I've thought through one hundred thousand times
words that we exchanged
and I think my instinct knows which way to go
I know you love me but do I still love you

Ground Control to Mrs Tom
Have you told him yet, that you can't go on
Can you hear me Mrs Tom
Can you want me Mrs Tom
Can you love me Mrs Tom
Can you

Here I lie in our council terrace
on top of the hill
Ground Control's here too
and there's nothing we can't do

Cysylltiadau Cymru

Cysylltiadau Cymru
gan gyrraedd allan
dros dir a môr

Cysylltiadau Cymraeg
galw atoch chi

Byddwn bob amser
yn cael ei gysylltu
ble bynnag yr ydych

Beth bynnag fo'ch cyfeiriad
bydd ein cysylltiad yn wir

Welsh Connections
(author translation)

Welsh connections
reaching out
o'er land and see

Welsh connections
calling out to you

We'll always
be connected
wherever you may be

Whatever your direction
our connection will hold true

In Dylan Thomas Summer School Blue

We come from different places
see in varying ways
carry unsuitable cases
act our one actor plays
we hear each other's stories
tell tall tales of our own
white lies and pretences
under cut over blown

Our words span the Atlantic
crash on either shore
phrases thrown like a forest
needle deep on the floor
our lines line-up beside us
stripes that shine with the stars
heart in the heat of a dragon
burnished craft of the Bards

Hillside sheep bleat our star signs in Welsh
destinies tangled in language and fleece
green as the grass stains engrained on our knees
croeso, araf, awen, ysgrifennu

→

State sidewinder ticks
time's J-crawling trails
hiraeth may hide in your flightcase
Cymru beneath fingernails
barddoniaeth steep your subconscious
Cymraeg's lullaby page
dragon's blood brothers and sisters
lead on each other's stage

Blue water, blue water, blue water
All we see all at sea all we see all our sea

Rydyn Ni Ar Goll Am Eiriau

Rydym yn dysgu Cymraeg
rydyn ni ar goll am eiriau
yn mynd drosodd yn lle dan
siarad rhy uchel yn lle rhy hir
ceisiwn dweud eich bod yn dal
ond dywedwn eich bod yn dew
ein bod yn gwybod gwin wrth gwrw

Yn ffodus rydyn ni mewn Clwb Llyfrau
(darllen, ddarllen)
a gall bob amser droi dros ddeilen newydd
(deilen, ddeilen)
Wrth ddarllen Cyfres Amdani mae
(geirfa, eirfa)
wastad gwelliannau i'n geirfa

Os yn sownd gallwn *(gallwn, allwn)*
ddyfeisio rhywbeth newydd *(rhywbeth, rywbeth)*
neu daflu gair Saesneg *(Saesneg, Sysneg)*
fel wheelbarrow i mewn *(wheelbarrow, wheelbarrow)*

Ond gan ein bod yn cyfarfod
yn yr hwyr mewn tafarn
gallwch fod yn sicr
ein bod yn gwybod gwin wrth gwrw

Ni ar goll am eiriau

We Are Lost For Words
(author translation)

We are learning Welsh
we are at a loss for words
going over when we mean under
talking too high when we mean long
trying to say you are tall
but say you are fat
we do know wine from beer

Fortunately we are in a Book Club
(read, read)
and can always turn over a new leaf
(leaf, leaf)
reading Cyfres Amdani is
(index, index)
constantly improving our vocabulary

If stuck we can always *(we can, we can)*
invent something new *(something, something)*
or throw in an English word *(English, English)*
like wheelbarrow *(wheelbarrow, wheelbarrow)*

But as we are meeting
in the evening in a pub
you can be certain
we do know wine from beer

We are lost for words

Swansea Girls *(chant)*

Swansea Girls
HAVE
straight hair and curls

Swansea Girls
KEEP
their flags unfurled

Swansea Girls
MAKE
love to boys and girls

Swansea Girls
ARE
the best girls in the world

The whole wide world
loves a SWANSEA GIRL!

Butter Cut

Is there such a post as Butter Butler?
Such a post holder should be super slick
so I raise my toast to Butter Butler
Butter Butler toast must be duper quick.

Melt into the arms of Butter Butler
trace the milky whey to sweet butter cream
succumb to the charms of Butter Butler
enthroned among the churns as Butter Queen.

There still rings a bell for Butter Butler
half a pounded dream of mid-butter's night
deep in Dingley Dell lies Butter Butler
no truth left to tell of our butter flight.

A bit of Butter Butler for a better life
or better bitter Butter Butler pulled the knife?

Life On Marzipan

Yellow planet of almond paste
Holding orbit in outer space
As you circle a golden sun
In the universe of Current Bun

Is this the end of the Bakewell scene
Put your fork through our Stollen dream
Demise of Patisserie too
And all wedding cakes divorcees

As the icing has saddening flaws
Though we've sieved it ten times or more
Like smearing two gooseberry fools
While you ask us to focus on

Nozzles piping dainty rose buds
Oh man, look at that wavy flow
It's the greasiest show
Take a look at that poor man
Icing up the wrong pie
Oh man, wonder if he'll ever know
He's in a nut shelling show
Is there life on Marzipan?

→

So our economy's tortured now
Always the lowly must draw the plough
Solzhenitsyn turns in his grave
'Cause Lenin's on sale again
Seaborne icing vermillion red
ECT now for all petrol heads
Cruel Britannia still ruled by clowns
Build back better on quagmire grounds
Still the icing has saddening flaws
Party cake in ten tiers ignored
They will write you a writ or ten
Try to force you to focus on

Nozzles piping dainty rose buds
Oh man, look at that wavy flow
Hear the Battenberg blow
Take a look at the poor man
Icing up the wrong pie
Oh man, wonder if he'll ever know
He's in a Bakery show
Is there life on Marzipan?

Star Jumper

'STAR JUMPER' glimpsed on a poster
as I dock in a space near the hall
fuels imaginary galactic adventures
weight free at light speed
through time leaps and worm holes

But the capsule displayed in the chamber
is not home to the gods that I thought
Mercury, Apollo and Artemis
are sadly quick slivers of silver
splashed down to Astro nought

Instead holding orbit a garment of wool
snowflakes, not stars, on the front
organic Faroese knitted cable
worn on TV by a Danish detective
not so much lunar as Lund

NASA forecast knitting on the ISS
Nyberg's interplanetary craft
but her films are of quilting
and sewn dinosaurs floating
no darn clickety-clack

Zero gravity suits crochet of chainmail
dark matter can hide in its gaps
and the zeal of heritage combatants suggests
on planets far away in the future
the Battle of Bosworth re-enacts

Helicave

Sacred stones no longer standing
but whirling above my head
grinding air to a downward plume
raising dust and this cave-home
where palm-paint hand-prints
mark time in ochre lifelines
on the naked innards of mountain
and gods' golden tongues flicker
to taste the dry sticks at my feet
hold back the black, breathe heat
until we rise as the sun into dawn.

High in bright pterodactyl-less sky
spinning stones spitting sharp sparks
I soar my helicave over icy peak
flit among goose-feather cloud
hover along wriggling snake of water
touch down in a niche of cliff
mouth agape to an unfamiliar vale
of disordered smell and uncollected taste
where I watch different colour skin
sing new sound to fresh rhythm
yet honour too gods' golden tongues.

Leary Call

Wine trodden by cows
as they herd it
through the grapevine
Alligator wins at poker
by seeing you later
Bike shed tears when
smoke gets in your eyes
Reading written right
through gaol house rock
Hungry sheep beetle to
manger knowing hay due
Six pistols under flint lock
and a key in the UK.
Grand flash if cats' eyes
don't do white lines

Fax You My Knickers

I've got a Sanaponic
X1-80 fax machine
in glorious technicolour
height of new technology
it's got aroma peripherals
it can transmit real smells
I can send my body odours
down your telephone line
Fax you my knickers?

Printing out on your A4
those scanty panties that I wore
black lace trimming, bows galore
those damper spots that you adore
receive
Fax you my knickers?

Download my sexy undies
into pulsing peeps of light
whisked across the country
like a laser through the sky
to a million subscribers
with scratch and sniff stains
receiving body odours
down their telephone lines
Fax you my knickers?

$\longrightarrow$

Wednesdays pink, Thursdays blue
Fridays panty-girdles too
water sported tights are new
a crutch to keep it up for you
Believe
Fax you my knickers?

New age of information
innovation breaking free
with multi-masturbation
conference facility
with your telecom adapter
you can input to my smalls
obtain my body odours
down your telephone line
Fax you my knickers?

It's hardened up your floppy disc
your overloaded RAM's at risk
the only constant thing is this
Men – and machines
are still sexist
Fax you my knickers?
UP YOURS!

Collect Stamps

Collect Stamps
Not just Penny Reds and Twopence Blues
Collect Stamps
The perforated ones you lick and go
Display
With colour lights at your place
Display
Crayon a title on upturned crates

It's so much fun
With gum and glue
And once they're applied
Won't slide
The thing that I like most
Is waiting for the post
If you should send me a nice stamp
I'd steam it with the kettle

Collect Stamps
Philately is cool
Collect Stamps
Precious paper jewels
Display
On special sheets cut to size
Display
In a nice album, a serious album

$\longrightarrow$

It's so much fun
With gum and glue
And once they're applied
Won't slide
And if you are a crook
They'll get you off the hook
Transfer your funds into hot stamps
And slip across the border
Collect Stamps
Not just Penny Reds and Twopence Blues
Display
In a nice album, a serious album
Collect Stamps, Stamps, Stamps

Power Tree

I planted a plethora of lightbulbs
before I finally got one to take
turned out I'd been potting them upside down
Gosh! The excitement on seeing
that first copper shoot
then blood dripping everywhere
from a grubby thumb caught
on a shard of leaf.
School always said I was light fingered

Big Pictures

For the big picture step back
from a painting
close to a window.
Moving art
breaks backs
however light
is captured.
Stay in the frame and you might
get carried away.

Roots I

To Burden

Remembering the things we did
once the canker rot set in
one turn ipso facto mashed my heart
though always I'll be true to you
venerate with all I am
exalt sweet love's pure sugar lick
gift and burden aeons alone may shift

Roots II

Tuber Done

Remembering the thing SWEDE did
Once the can CARROT set in
One TURNIP so facto MASHED my heart
Though always I'll BEETROOT chew
Venerate with all I YAM
Exalt sweet love's pure sch GARLIC
Gift and bird ONIONS alone may shift

Relative

My half brother
is propped in the hall
oozing into the wallpaper
by a rack of left shoes
his NHS glasses
dangling.

My step mother
is sitting by the front door
holding a bottle of milk.

At the back door
I see my two faced sister
and wonder
if she is leaving
or entering.

I'm the black sheep
of the family
tangled up in wool.

Action Dad

Bringing me a growling teddy bear from the Black Forest
Beating your Tarzan chest in tiger stripe swimming trunks
Teaching me to chop wood with an axe
Leaping the garden fence to rescue me
Halting the match when I collapsed
Standing alongside at my wedding
Holding my shaking hand
Kissing me goodnight
Being there
Being

.

Sense of Loss

Although Mum always said
I was born short of sense
I assumed there'd be plenty to last
but I've way over felt
caused my feeling to melt
perhaps my last touching date has just passed.

I know eyesight fades
we're prepared with good aids
spectacles, lenses and laser
but I've heard no one reveal
you lose grip on your feel
from nights on the tactiles eraser.

Hearing disappearing
has brought new engineering
ear trumpets are now small as pips
but through all magazines
not once have I seen
a top-10 list of new finger tips.

I've even heard tell
of folks losing their smell
and their taste, which is close in connection
but not to sit on the fence
this running out of a sense
only four out of five get a mention.

→

At the doctor's surgery
the touch-screen defeated me
you can't imagine how I don't feel
the NHS helpline
said 'touch-tone' three times
then diagnosed that I'm not real.

So I went down the shops
and checked every box
but they were virtually all of them senseless
just one tasty surprise
two sights for sore eyes
and a fraudulent MPs expenses.

In Boots my prescription
couldn't find any friction
I tried all that the chemist dispenses
even sex has turned sour
I have staying power
but can no longer come to my senses.

I blame the kids
with their computer whizz
and lingo that seems double Dutch
my nephews and nieces
made me fall quite to pieces
when they whispered:
"Auntie's so out of touch."

Another Ill Wind

You can't get khaki car keys
but you can get a khaki car key holder
I lost my duck key
now my Khaki Campbell won't quack
it seems my luck took a plunge
with a clockwork duck a l'orange.

You cannot be serious in cerise
but you can get cereals in series
CoCo Pops through Cornflakes to Rice Crispies
but you said my variety pack
has lost its crackle and popped its snap
little wonder my Khaki Campbell won't quack!

Love Bomb

I know she means business
by the Molotov cocktail
feather in her cap,
slow-burn fuse
fizzing behind dark eyes
and unguarded explosion
of a smile.

People sea-part
before her stride,
cacophony cans silent
in my ears,
music and heartbeat throb
as I brace for her kiss
and the

BOOM!

Paradise With You

All the milk and honey is gone
no meat in the stew
wolves howling at our door
rent's way overdue
but there's still a smile on my face
'cause I'm lying here next to you
it's another day in paradise
if I spend it with you

We spend our lives side by side
on brighter days and blue
hand in hand we take our stand
pull each other through
push all the troubles there are in the world
down Tomorrow Avenue
it's another day in paradise
if I spend it with you

Longer shadows, aches and pains
age ravages through
not gone to seed, but all we need
bare necessities of Baloo
with fingers and thumbs we count our sums
everything adds up to two
it's another day in paradise
if I spend it with you

$\rightarrow$

Down the line we'll run out of time
will I go first or you
body gone, spirit soars on
we limped and then we flew
one thing to confess within our caress
true love is life's super glue
all my days are in paradise
when I spend them with you

Now I've Got A Reason

You rescued me
from the cat's mouth of life
purchased time
to heal my wings
accepted me
as lover and wife
revealed the sun
returned reason
to sing

Tree Call

On Lonesome Pine Trail
heartwood arrows pry open
lovesick sycamore

All The Words I Never Said

You held my hand like it was sheathed in leaf gold
I'm told
love hold
brought back a brown bear from a German forest
so proud
still growls

First home a house across the fields with no road
hand-me-down furniture by wheelbarrow load
I was three when you were late for dinner
climb to the roof ridge that I don't remember
on high
I spy

All the songs I never sang to you
all the words I never said.

You drove a lorry sat me on the gearbox
all warm
no harm
built our treehouse from a flight of old stairs
our realm
green elm

→

Swam in the river beat your chest like Tarzan
gave me pyjamas with the moon and stars on
dunked your Custard Creams and Jammy Dodgers
sang us a song recorded by Roy Rogers
'A Four
Legged Friend'

All the songs I never sang to you
all the words I never said.

Your maroon Corsair took us to the seaside
played *Pubs and Garages* to speed the drive time
taught me to kick a ball and skin a rabbit
swing an axe, mow hay and stack it
times past
too fast

All the songs I never sang to you
all the words I never said

All these songs I never sang to you
all the words I wish I'd said.

Legacy Circus

The children I leave behind are words
Words that hold my thoughts and dreams
Dreams of love, nightmares of sorrow
Sorrow shared on white in black
Black as tea that's steeped too long
Long shadows strained in shady lines
Lines that catch all fish in rhyme
Rhyme and rhythm, song and tune
Tune into the wavering moon
Moon Boots wading bird to sing
Sing the rhyming fish song worm
Worm into the mind and spirit
Spirit spit that foams the waves
Waves goodbye from alien climes
Climbs the final step to fly
Fly away all lines are cut
Cut and paste away my words
Words the children I leave behind

One Dark Night

You were only children
Filled with light of youth
Stories yet to be written
Promise still to fulfil
Smiles of delight for the future
Happiness burned in your eyes
Don't be afraid of the dark
I will hold your hand

Mothers and daughters and freedom
Stars in this blackest of skies
Arena of dancing and music
Echoes with joyful young lives
Don't be afraid of the dark
I will hold your hand

Share (*Round*)

Shout
shout it out
so there's no doubt
stand up and shout

Pain
falls like rain
in my brain
again and again

Pain
cuts like glass
makes my tears splash
it lasts and lasts

Donna, Anthony, Auntie Pat and my Nan
Charlie, Jenny, Auntie Joan and my Gran
John, Alan, two Uncle Bills, Shirley and Nance
Babber, Bambi, my Grandfather and my Dad

Shout
shout it out
so there's no doubt
stand up and shout

$\rightarrow$

Pain
falls like rain
in my brain
again and again

Pain
cuts like glass
makes my tears splash
it lasts and lasts

(insert names here .....)

Shout
(etc ......)

Elegy To Mr Walker-Petts

Walter Walker-Petts
was a dear friend of mine
he lived in a pile
down the Axminster line
a luminary trusted with secrets
who knew how to knot a good fly
his matter-of-fact style
belied rugged looks
and when on a roll
had a wit that could floor you

Some thought him hard
said his heart was harder
than nothing or no-one could melt
but I know love trod him down
years of being walked over
wore away self-esteem
left emotions under felt
yet he was quick to pick up
on anything afoot
recognise just how things lay

$\rightarrow$

Although life was plush
he kept working class charm
always ready to spin a yarn
I'll never forget those Burns' Nights
the scars are still with me today
so let's raise a glass to Walter
and one final night on the tiles
a send-off for the last of the tuft guys
Walter Walker-Petts
Good Buy!

Falling Apart With You

All I wanted
was a new refrain
another chance
to sing my song to you
playful music
notes that fall like rain
renew our world
brighten up the blue

Each day
opens clean and fresh
blank page
awaiting your paint brush
make your time
no need to rush
shake the world
disturb the dust
strike your metal
never let it rust

$\rightarrow$

We both
straddle the same broom
each night
howling at the moon
reface the music
reclaim that tune
take our chants
to the last saloon
share a basket
under one balloon

We'll all
fall apart one day
return
to water air and clay
each grain of sand
that falls is gone
another note
played from our song
keep on singing
while your voice is strong

Until you hear the angels
sing along

Stricken

On grey days you wear her shawl
as if that could cover all
the clout of her on your shoulders

Beneath, your head bows
lower than the lonely low of cows
in long snuffed glow of her candleholders

On grey days you wear her shawl
as if it would enfold the haul
of emptiness that glitters your eyes

Embosomed, your effort wastes
all life bereft of time and taste
in the silent echo of her swallowed cries

On grey days you wear her shawl
as if it should envelop the shoal
of memories that swim in your tears

Within, your spirit depletes
as you diminish inside this shawl of grief
on the grey days of her missing years

Expertease

This afterlife
is no second breakfast
although a faint scent
of burned toast
taints tortured air
and tings the tang
of thick-cut citrus
against my tongue
as crunching
eggshell echoes
tickle an eardrum
in reggae rhythm
tinged with a hue
of the blue/greens
smooth and tangled
as intestines

Mycycle

Tomorrow
I will stand tall
raise arms to the sun
dance in the wind
shelter from rain
nestle with nuthatch and pine martin
rattle with woodpecker
feed squirrel
hide moth
decorate with lichen.

Today
I curl
flesh and bone
an intern
learning to subside
in the entwining
draw of roots
from the sapling
planted
above my head.

Death Is Like A Box Of Chocolates

Walnut Whipping
Vanilla Evisceration
Butterscotch Stoning
Gas Chamber Cappuccino
Hazelnut Hanging
Lethal Lemon Injection
Keelhauling Caramel
Turkish Decapitation
Black Forest Burning
Strawberry Strychnine
Firing Squad Fudge
Coconut Crucifixion
Passion Fruit Flaying
Guillotine Nougat
Electric Chair Cherry
Coffee Cremation
Blackberry Burial
Death By Chocolate

ooOOOoo

Afterword by Dominic Williams

There is some sense of continuity between **Seeds from a Dandelion** and this, Karen Gemma Brewer's second collection **Dancing in the Sun**. It is another comprehensive volume, of over 100 pages and as you may expect, addresses a solid set of issues, contemporary and universal. It is perhaps the contemporary; both its impact upon the poet's composition and my reading; that flavours the collection, if not with a sense of resignation, then a certain melancholic acceptance. Voicing thought about such dense topics as politics, gender politics, global warming, love and death is always lightened and awarded easy access by Brewer's great sense of fun and love of playing with words.

I have become familiar with recent public deliveries of poems such as **Important Questions on Self-Driving Cars, Bouquet of Giraffes** and **Monster Love Monster** all great examples of Brewer's surrealist humour, accomplished word-play and are invitations to the reader to more carefully investigate and appreciate her creative skills and to listen closer to their own social conscience. The in-your-face poems about global warming and politics **Drumming In Your Ears** or **We Don't Want You In** for example are balanced by others that draw the reader in with literary techniques, offering easy and subtle laughs and chuckles followed by that epiphanic moment.

The moon features in several poems, of course in **Lunar Seer** and **Lunartrix,** in which I love the poet's stated position of 'one foot in a crater'. Much later a reference to 'howling at the moon' occurs toward the end of the collection in **Falling Apart With You**. This is the third of three poems that I feel truly knit the collection together in a deeply personal way. The title poem **Dancing In The Sun** appears quite early in the book and is seemingly complete in its total season cycle, but **Now I've Got A Reason** is a short poem that is, of itself, an epiphanic moment that naturally connects to **Falling Apart With You** in a way that creates a far more all-inclusive sense of a relationship.

As the director of the Dylan Thomas Summer School, I have a natural affinity for **In Dylan Thomas Sumer School Blue** but, also, a unique understanding in the reading of this piece of Brewer's insightful wit and intense empathy with a community of peers. Other personal favourites include **Menagerine** and the page spindling **Thin** which includes the word 'semaphwoar'. So many poems are, it seems, written just for the fun of themselves, the reader seeks beyond the puns, the alliteration for a deeper meaning when sometimes they are just gifts, touchstones of joy and identification with the reader, **Leary Call** left me with so many pop-culture references and the inevitable re-surfacing of personal memories.

Non-stick Pandemonium is another fine use of humour and wordsmithery to capture the absolute despair of late pandemic and early post-pandemic. The ability to laugh in our most desperate situations is what allows hope and that hope is given its greatest support by profound love. Quite late in the collection is another of several loose sections of themed poems: the 'family' section. There is a beautiful and brilliant juxtaposition of **Action Dad**; a condensed poem that slowly fades to less but more vital words, the last 'Being'; with **All the Words I Never Said,** a longer poem, but no less carefully and compassionately crafted, gently laying out stanzas that could be heard like distant echoes between the lines of the earlier deliberately sparse poem. I am a great fan of Brewer on-stage and hear her voice so clearly in many of these poems, a very distinct poetic voice but also in my head a distinct performance voice.

Notes

Lunar Seer the layout aims to mimic reflection of moon on sea

Menagerine was first published in *Talisman* and owes some debt to Edward Lear from who I learned at an early age, when you can't find the right word, make one up

Arm A Nag is an anagram of anagram

Lunartrix was written for and performed by the folk duo *Raker's Moon* to music by Paul Hayes

Thin was written to fill a narrow space in Lampeter's *Grapevine*

Drumming In Your Ears was written for a duet performance with Llinos Belcher which circumstance has delayed

Dancing In The Sun was written and recorded for *'Equinox'* (*Showboat TV 2021*)

Non-Stick Pandemonium was published in *A Fish Rots From The Head: A Poetic and Political Wake* (Culture Matters 2022) and an earlier version was published by I Am Not A Silent Poet (2019)

Candyfloss & Brandysnaps was first published by I Am Not A Silent Poet (2018)

Just Another Hole In The Head the phrase *raisin eye* is borrowed from Dawn Morgan's poem *The Royal Gout* published in her collection *Blood and Other Elements* (Rack Press 2018)

Number Nineteen Twenty Twenty Division Blues was published in *Talisman* and *Seeds from A Dandelion - addition edition* (Cowry Publishing 2021)

Down was first published in *Swansea Poetry Slam Anthology* (Frequency House 2021)

I'll Never Stay At The Dorchester was written for the Sultan of Brunei in support of the Dorchester Hotel Chain protests, published in *Gwrthryfel Uprising an anthology of radical poetry from contemporary Wales* (Culture Matters 2022) and, translated into Italian by Virginia Vitale and Gerardina Fruncillo, in *Correnti Incrociate 2* (Mosaïque Press 2022)

Monster Love Monster was published in *Light After Snow* (Peter, Bridge and Steffan 2019) and *Seeds from A Dandelion - addition edition* (Cowry Publishing 2021)

Treasure's Hunt was first performed at the *Edinburgh Festival Fringe* on a show with John Collins

Odd Space was inspired by David Bowie

In Dylan Thomas Summer School Blue was written and performed at the *Dylan Thomas Summer School 2019*. Translation of Welsh: croeso araf awen ysgrifennu = welcome slow muse write; hiraeth = longing; Cymru = Wales; barddoniaeth = poetry; Cymraeg = Welsh.

Rydyn Ni Ar Goll Am Eiriau was written for *Clwb Darllen Cymraeg Rhos Yr Hafod* and performed at the *Eisteddfod Genedlaethol Ceredigion 2022*

Swansea Girls (chant) was first performed on Radio Tircoed and first published in *Talisman*

Life On Marzipan was inspired by David Bowie

Star Jumper Detective Chief Inspector Sara Lund is a character in Scandi Noir 'The Killing,' played by Sofie Grabol, famed for her Faroe Isle knitted jumpers. Karen Nyberg, the 50th woman in space, was reportedly planning to knit on the International Space Station but video evidence of her extra-terrestrial handicrafts is of a sewn quilt and soft toy dinosaur

Helicave what if standing stones are discarded helicopter blades previously used to fly caves from one mountain range to another?

Leary Call from parental influence to teenage years an unfinished poem I hope to add lines to all my life. Feel free to add your own

Fax You My Knickers was first performed at the *Edinburgh Festival Fringe* on a show with Friz Frizzle

Collect Stamps was inspired by David Bowie

Relative was first published in *Light After Snow* (Peter, Bridge and Steffan 2019) and *Seeds from A Dandelion - addition edition* (Cowry Publishing 2021)

Another Ill Wind is an update of the poem *Ill Wind* published in *Seeds from A Dandelion* (Cowry Publishing 2017). Swansea clubbers will know the correct pronunciation of the title

Now I've Got A Reason takes its title from a repeated line in the 1977 Sex Pistols song *Holidays In The Sun*

One Dark Night was written in May 2017 following the Manchester Arena bombing

Death Is Like A Box Of Chocolates the title is a misquote from the film *Forrest Gump (Paramount: 1994)*

Smile, be happy, have fun :-D